First published in this format 2015

Text and photos: Jen Carreiro,
   of SomethingTurquoise.com
Editor: Timothy Stobierski
Copy editor: Betty Christiansen
Illustrations: Andrew Logan Wanke
Design: Kimberly Adis
Layout: Lynne Phillips

The Taunton Press
Inspiration for hands-on living®

The Taunton Press, Inc., 63 South Main Street
PO Box 5506, Newtown, CT 06470-5506
e-mail: tp@taunton.com

Threads® is a trademark of The Taunton Press, Inc.,
registered in the U.S. Patent and Trademark Office.

The following names/manufacturers appearing in
Felt Flowers are trademarks: Hobby Lobby®, JoAnn
Fabric and Craft Stores®, Martha Stewart Crafts®,
Michaels®, Mod Podge®

Library of Congress Cataloging-in-Publication Data

Carreiro, Jen, author.
  Felt flowers : designs for year-round blooms / Jen
Carreiro.
      pages cm
  Includes bibliographical references.
  Audience: Age 13.
  Audience: Grade 9 to 12.
  ISBN 978-1-63186-349-3
1. Fabric flowers--Juvenile literature. 2. Felt work--
Juvenile literature. I. Title.
  TT890.5.C37 2015
  745.594'3--dc23
                                2015032691

Printed in the United States of America
10 9 8 7 6 5 4 3 2 1

Contents

Ravishing Rose

Gorgeous long-stem roses can be one of the most expensive flowers to purchase and, sadly, can be enjoyed only for a short time. Creating these sought-after blooms using felt will ensure years of enjoyment. The best part is that they can be created in any color you want!

FELT PER FLOWER

9-in. by 12-in. colored felt for petals

1-in. by 1-in. green felt for flower base

TEMPLATES TO CUT PER FLOWER

8 petals of Petal 1

8 petals of Petal 2

4 small Inner Petals

1 Flower Base

NOTIONS

Patterns (see p. 28)

Scissors

Wire cutters

Hot-glue gun (or strong glue of your choice)

14-in. length of 18-gauge floral wire

SHOWN IN

Petals: burgundy, sugar plum, and rose

Flower Base: sage

Medium Leaves (see p. 26)

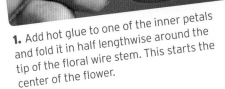

1. Add hot glue to one of the inner petals and fold it in half lengthwise around the tip of the floral wire stem. This starts the center of the flower.

2. Hot-glue the remaining 3 inner petals together in a row, overlapping them by ¼ in.

3. Hot-glue the end of the row of 3 petals to the center petal.

4. Wrap the row of 3 petals all the way around and hot-glue in place. The center of the rose is now complete.

continued on p. 6

5

5. Working with one large petal at a time, add hot glue to the bottom half and wrap it around the center.

6. To achieve volume within the design, slightly pinch the petal while you are gluing it.

Accessorize

1 or 2 rose blooms are an easy way to jazz up a Valentine's Day gift—just glue or tape them onto the package!

7. Switch back and forth between adding the two petal shapes to achieve a natural variation, working evenly around the rose and overlapping one petal with a previous petal's edge.

8. Cut a slit in the base. Thread the base on the wire stem. Add hot glue to the center of the base, then wrap it around to the bottom of the flower, pinching it as the glue is drying to finish the design.

Appealing Anemone

This beautifully sweet anemone design is one of the easiest flowers to create! The impressive little bloom only has nine petals and a fanned center that can be finished in a flash. Show off your creative style and build an entire bouquet in less than two hours.

FELT PER FLOWER

4-in. by 9-in. colored felt for petals

3/4-in. by 3-in. rectangle of black felt for center

1-in. by 1-in. green felt for flower base

1-cm black felt ball

TEMPLATES TO CUT PER FLOWER

9 Petals

1 Center

1 Flower Base

NOTIONS

Patterns (see p. 28)

Scissors

Wire cutters

Hot-glue gun (or strong glue of your choice)

14-in length of 18-gauge floral wire

SHOWN IN

Petals: oats

Flower Center and Ball: graphite

Flower Base: fern

Large Leaves (see p. 25)

1. Snip a small X in the felt ball.

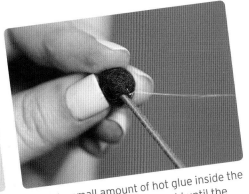

2. Add a small amount of hot glue inside the X and insert the floral wire. Hold until the glue has dried.

3. Snip 1/8-in. cuts across one side of the felt rectangle, leaving at least 1/4 in. uncut along one long edge.

4. Add a line of hot glue to the uncut edge of the rectangle and wrap it tightly and completely around the felt ball base. Fan out the cut pieces to form the center of the flower.

continued on p. 8

Accessorize

You can turn this flower into a quick little hair clip by snipping the floral wire and gluing the base of the flower to your clip. Play around with the flower's position before gluing to ensure you like how it will look.

5. Working with one petal at a time, add a small amount of hot glue to the bottom half of a petal and adhere it to the center, pinching to secure. Add a total of 4 petals evenly around the center.

6. Working with one petal at a time, hot-glue the remaining 5 petals underneath the first 4 petals, positioning them in a natural way and overlapping the edges.

7. Cut a slit in the center of the flower base, thread the stem through it, and add hot glue as shown. Slide the base underneath the petals.

8. Pinch the flower base to the petals as the glue is drying to finish the design.

Tip

Cut multiple petals with ease by creating your pattern out of felt instead of paper. Felt is much easier to hold while cutting.

Radiant Ranunculus

Known for its layers of soft, undulating petals, the ranunculus makes a fabulous felt flower. Versatile and unique in shape, this flower can be created in any size you'd like, so you might want to make multiples! Don't forget to make a few darling ranunculus flower buds as well.

Ranunculus

FELT PER FLOWER
9-in. by 12-in. colored felt piece for petals

1-in. by 1-in. green felt piece for flower base

TEMPLATES TO CUT PER FLOWER
27 Petals, ranging in size from ¾ in. to 1½ in.

1 Flower Base

NOTIONS
Patterns (see p. 28)

Scissors

Wire cutters

Hot-glue gun (or strong glue of your choice)

14-in length of 18-gauge floral wire

SHOWN IN
Petals: rose and mulberry

Flower Base: fern

Small Leaves (see p. 27)

1. Cut out 27 petals for this flower, ranging in size from ¾ in. to 1½ in. (the exact number of each size of petal will be up to you). The pattern on p. 28 is 1½ in. in diameter; use it as a guide to create smaller petals. The smaller circles are for the center of the flower, and they gradually get larger as they move out. Snip a hole in the center of the smallest petal.

2. Thread the smallest petal onto the wire, leaving about ½ in. sticking out, and add hot glue.

3. Pinch the petal into an X shape as shown to form the center of the flower.

4. Working with one petal at a time, add hot glue to the bottom half of each and press underneath the center.

continued on p. 12

Tip

If you're looking to arrange these beauties in a clear vase, add a few leaves to the flower stems themselves for a more natural appearance.

5. Continue adding petals, creating the flower. Make sure to start with the smallest petals and work up in size to the largest.

6. As you apply a petal, overlap one edge of the previous petal and gently press until the glue is dry.

7. Cut a slit in the center of the flower base, thread onto the wire, and add hot glue. Press the base around the bottom, pinching it as the glue is drying to finish the design.

Ranunculus Bud

FELT PER FLOWER BUD
1-in. by 1-in. colored felt piece for petal

1-in. by 1-in. green felt piece for leaf

TEMPLATES TO CUT PER BUD
1 Bud Petal

1 Bud Leaf

NOTIONS
Patterns (see p. 28)

Scissors

Wire cutters

Hot-glue gun (or strong glue of your choice)

14-in length of 20-gauge floral wire

SHOWN IN
Bud Petals: rose and mulberry

Bud Leaf: fern

1. Snip a little notch in the center of both the petal and the leaf.

2. Thread the petal onto the wire, leaving about ½ in. sticking out.

3. Add hot glue to one tip of the petal.

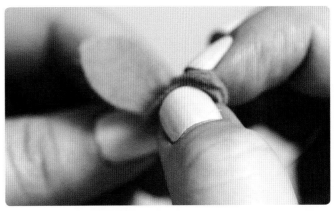

4. Press the hot-glued petal and the petal opposite it together.

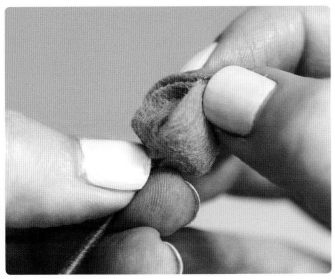

5. Hot-glue and press the remaining 2 petal ends together, forming the flower bud.

6. Thread the leaf onto the wire and add hot glue to each tip of the leaf.

7. Press the leaf tips around the flower bud.

Accessorize

It's easy to turn these blooms into beautiful accessories. Simply glue one or two flowers onto a clip that you can then attach to your purse or even to the top of your shoes.

Terrific Tulip

Tulips are beautifully simple and can quickly put a smile on your face with their presence. They are the flower that embodies springtime, but these sweet felt versions can be enjoyed no matter what season it is. This simple design takes only a few minutes to create and will make a unique impact in any arrangement.

FELT PER FLOWER
4-in. by 9-in. colored felt piece for petals

3-cm felt ball

1½-in. by 1½-in. green felt piece for flower base

TEMPLATES TO CUT PER FLOWER
6 Petals

1 Flower Base

NOTIONS
Patterns (see p. 29)

Scissors

Wire cutters

Hot-glue gun (or strong glue of your choice)

14-in length of 18-gauge floral wire

SHOWN IN
Petals: grapefruit

Felt Ball: almond

Flower Base: fern

1. Snip a small X in the felt ball.

2. Add a small amount of hot glue inside the X.

3. Insert the floral wire into the X, and hold until the glue has dried.

4. Make a ½-in. snip in the center of the bottom of each petal; this is very important for the folding of each petal.

5. Working with one petal at a time, add a small amount of hot glue to the bottom of the petal just to the left of the snip.

6. Quickly pull and fold the other side of the petal bottom on top of the hot glue, pleating the petal so it forms a cup. Hold the pleated area between your fingers until the glue dries.

continued on p. 16

Tip

I use fabric-wrapped floral wire (also called "string-wrapped") for most of these designs because it adds to the softness of the flower stem. It is available at most big box craft retailers, including online stores.

15

7. Repeat for all 6 petals.

8. Working with one petal at a time, add a small amount of hot glue to the inside of each petal cup where the edges overlap.

Accessorize

You can turn these tulips into easy gifts simply by replacing the floral wire with a pen. Glue the bloom on top, wrap the body of the pen in floral tape, and you've got an adorable accessory!

9. Hold the stem with one hand as you press a petal cup onto the felt ball with the other.

10. Evenly add the first 3 petals around the felt ball center and then follow the directions to add the remaining 3 petals. Overlap the edges of the 3 inner petals when you place the 3 outer petals.

11. Cut a slit in the center of the flower base, thread it onto the wire, and add hot glue. Press the base around the bottom, pinching it as the glue is drying to finish the design.

Lovely Lily

These large and lovely blooms will steal the spotlight in any felt arrangement as they do in real life! Wire added to the back of each petal allows you to mold and shape them as you please. Lilies are naturally found in many different colors, so get creative with this design.

FELT PER FLOWER

6-in. by 9-in. colored felt piece for petals

2-in. by 2-in. felt piece for center

½-in. by 1½-in. felt piece for stamen

1-in. by 1-in. green felt piece for flower base

TEMPLATES TO CUT PER FLOWER

6 Petals

3 Stamen

1 Flower Center

1 Flower Base

NOTIONS

Patterns (see p. 29)

Scissors

Wire cutters

Hot-glue gun (or strong glue of your choice)

Three 14-in. lengths of 20-gauge floral wire

Six 5-in. strips of 18-gauge floral wire

Floral tape

SHOWN IN

Petals: pink

Stamen: seaside

Flower Centers: linen, butter, and rose

Medium Leaves (see p. 26)

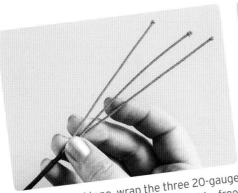

1. Using floral tape, wrap the three 20-gauge floral wires together, leaving about 4 in. free at the top. Stretch the tape as you use it, which helps it stick to itself.

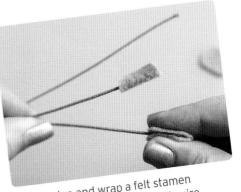

2. Hot-glue and wrap a felt stamen lengthwise onto the top of each wire.

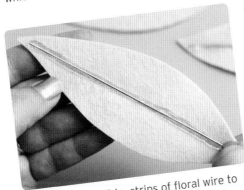

3. Hot-glue the 5-in. strips of floral wire to the center backside of each flower petal. This will allow you to mold the flower into its curved shape.

4. Cut a small slit in the center of the flower center and thread it onto the wire. Slide it up until there is about 1 in. between the flower center and the top of the stamens.

continued on p. 19

Accessorize

These lilies make wonderful and memorable boutonnieres for the prom or any other big day. Just snip a lily below the flower base and glue it to a pin back for a memento that will last forever! Add some leaves for extra dimension.

Tip

In nature, lilies have gorgeous coloring. Try hand-painting natural details on each petal before you assemble the flower. Search online for lily images to get ideas.

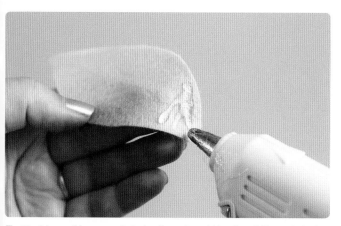

5. Working with one petal at a time, bend the tip of the petal at a 90-degree angle. Add hot glue to the bottom portion of the petal, on the side without the wire (the wire will sit under each petal).

6. Hot-glue the first 3 petals onto the wire evenly, pinching the bottom as they are added until the glue dries.

7. Then hot-glue the remaining 3 petals evenly underneath the first 3 petals, again pinching the bottoms in place.

8. Add hot glue to the center where the petals meet the wire and press the center down into it.

9. Cut a small slit in the center of the flower base and thread it onto the wire. Slide it up the bottom of the flower, add hot glue, and pinch as the glue is drying to finish the design.

10. Bend and arrange the petals as you please.

Harmonious Hydrangea

This magnificent flower boasts around 60 blooms, but it is incredibly easy to create. Add just one of these flowers to an arrangement of other flowers to create wonderful volume and texture. Hydrangeas are found in many different colors, some blooms having multiple colors within them, but they are best known for their gorgeous shades of blue.

FELT PER FLOWER
12-in. by 18-in. colored felt piece for petals

TEMPLATES TO CUT PER FLOWER
60 Petals
60 Flower Centers

NOTIONS
Patterns (see p. 29)

Scissors

Wire cutters

Hot-glue gun (or strong glue of your choice)

35 pieces of 22-gauge floral wire

Floral tape

Needle-nose pliers

Optional hole punch

SHOWN IN
Petals: periwinkle and violet
Large Leaves (see p. 25)

1. Hold all 35 of the 22-gauge floral wires together and wrap with floral tape, leaving around 4 in. free at the top. Stretch the tape as you use it, which helps it stick to itself.

2. Bend and separate each of the 35 wires.

3. Using needle-nose pliers, bend the top ⅛ in. at the end of each wire at a 90-degree angle.

4. Snip a hole in the center of 35 of the petals.

continued on p. 22

Tip

Using a regular hole punch to cut out the tiny flower centers is much easier than cutting them out by hand. One end of the felt might stick to the punch, but you can snip it off with scissors.

5. Working with one snipped petal at a time, thread the wire through the felt petal and let the 90-degree bend rest on the top of it.

6. Add a tiny spot of hot glue to the place where the wire meets the petal.

7. Cover the hot glue with a flower center, sealing the petal to the wire. Do this to all 35 wires.

8. Hot-glue the flower centers to the remaining 25 petals.

9. Hot-glue the remaining petals to petals secured on the wires to build the fullness of the flower. Try to have as little space showing through the petals as possible.

10. Hot-glue some petals on top of other petals, some underneath, and some in between.

Accessorize

Make a few extra petals and glue a couple to a greeting card for a personal touch, or even place one on a ring blank for a quick addition to your jewelry box!

Limitless Leaves

Leaves are so fun to make because the shapes found in nature are super easy to replicate with felt. These three shapes have been designed to blend perfectly with all six of the flowers included in this booklet. Make yours in any color of green felt you would like, then mix and match with your favorite felt flower!

Large Leaf

LARGE LEAF
2½-in. by 4-in. green felt piece per leaf

LEAVES PER WIRE
1 to 2

NOTIONS
Pattern (see p. 29)

Scissors

Wire cutters

Hot-glue gun (or strong glue of your choice)

12-in. length of 20-gauge floral wire

SHOWN IN
Fern

1. Add hot glue to the backside of each leaf.

2. Cut a piece of wire to fit the length of the leaf, plus an additional 9 in., and hot-glue it in place. You can add 1 or 2 large leaves to each wire.

3. If you want to be able to bend and shape the leaves themselves, you need to glue the wire across the entire length of the backside. If you are creating a really large leaf, you can even add multiple sections of wire to the backside for added stability.

continued on p. 26

Medium Leaf

MEDIUM LEAF
1½-in. by 3-in. green felt piece per leaf

LEAVES PER WIRE
1 to 3

NOTIONS
Pattern (see p. 29)

Scissors

Wire cutters

Hot-glue gun (or strong glue of your choice)

12-in. length of 22-gauge floral wire

SHOWN IN
Sage

1. Add hot glue to the backside of each leaf.

2. Cut a piece of wire to fit the length of the leaf, plus an additional 9 in., and hot-glue it in place.

3. You can add 2 to 3 medium leaves to each wire (space them naturally). Try overlapping the leaves for some interesting texture.

Small Leaf

SMALL LEAF
1-in. by 2-in. green felt piece per leaf

LEAVES PER WIRE
3 to 5

NOTIONS
Pattern (see p. 29)

Scissors

Wire cutters

Hot-glue gun (or strong glue of your choice)

12-in. length of 22-gauge floral wire

SHOWN IN
Olive

Accessorize

You can use these leaves to create a whimsical crown for your little one's make-believe play. Just create a ring with floral wire that is big enough to sit atop the head, wrap with floral tape, and glue on the leaves. Add a variety of flowers to really kick things up!

1. Add hot glue to the backside of the leaf.

2. Cut a piece of wire to fit the length of the leaf, plus an additional 9 in., and hot-glue it in place.

3. You can add 3 to 5 small leaves to each wire. Space the leaves along the wire as desired.

4. To make a larger leaf branch, take 5 pieces of 22-gauge wire and wrap them with floral tape. Fan the wires out and hot-glue 1 or 2 leaves to each wire.

Felt Flower Patterns

All patterns shown at 100%.

Ravishing Rose

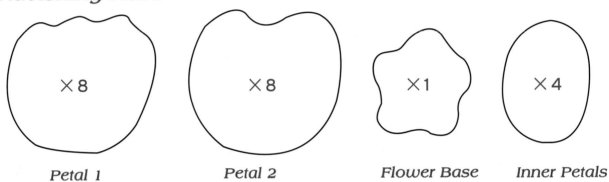

Petal 1 ×8   Petal 2 ×8   Flower Base ×1   Inner Petals ×4

Appealing Anemone

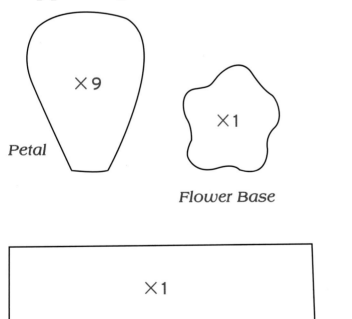

Petal ×9

Flower Base ×1

Center ×1

Radiant Ranunculus

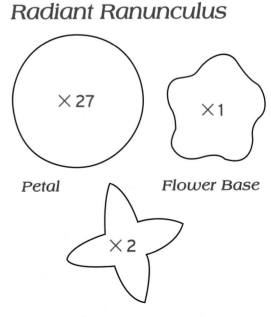

Petal ×27

Flower Base ×1

Bud Petal/Bud Leaf ×2

Terrific Tulip

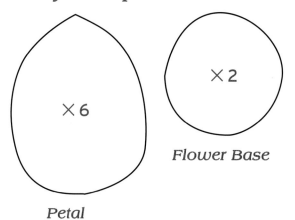

×6

Petal

×2

Flower Base

Harmonious Hydrangea

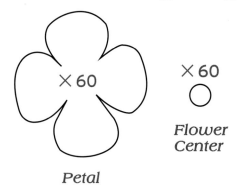

×60

Petal

×60

Flower Center

Limitless Leaves

Lovely Lily

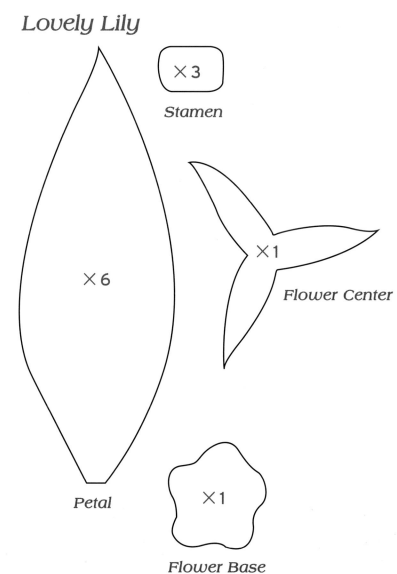

×3

Stamen

×6

Petal

×1

Flower Center

×1

Flower Base

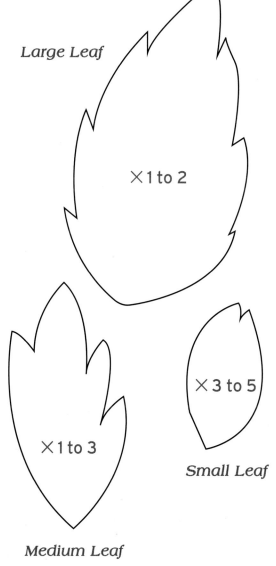

Large Leaf

×1 to 2

×1 to 3

Medium Leaf

×3 to 5

Small Leaf

Resources

Michaels®
North America's largest specialty retailer of arts and crafts for the hobbyist.
www.michaels.com

Hobby Lobby®
Retailer for arts and crafts supplies, both online and with more than 500 store locations.
www.hobbylobby.com

A.C. Moore
Arts & Crafts superstores in the eastern United States from Maine to Florida.
www.acmoore.com

JoAnn Fabric and Craft Stores®
Fabric and craft stores.
www.joann.com

Etsy
An online marketplace where you can sell and buy handmade items and supplies.
www.etsy.com

All felt and felt balls from BenzieDesign.
www.etsy.com/shop/BenzieDesign

Painted mason jars from KA Styles Mason Jar Décor.
www.etsy.com/shop/KAStylesMasonJars

Metric Equivalents

One inch equals approximately 2.54 centimeters. To convert inches to centimeters, multiply the figure in inches by 2.54 and round off to the nearest half centimeter, or use the chart below, whose figures are rounded off (1 centimeter equals 10 millimeters).

⅛ in. = 3 mm	9 in. = 23 cm
¼ in. = 6 mm	10 in. = 25.5 cm
⅜ in. = 1 cm	12 in. = 30.5 cm
½ in. = 1.3 cm	14 in. = 35.5 cm
⅝ in. = 1.5 cm	15 in. = 38 cm
¾ in. = 2 cm	16 in. = 40.5 cm
⅞ in. = 2.2 cm	18 in. = 45.5 cm
1 in. = 2.5 cm	20 in. = 51 cm
2 in. = 5 cm	21 in. = 53.5 cm
3 in. = 7.5 cm	22 in. = 56 cm
4 in. = 10 cm	24 in. = 61 cm
5 in. = 12.5 cm	25 in. = 63.5 cm
6 in. = 15 cm	36 in. = 92 cm
7 in. = 18 cm	45 in. = 114.5 cm
8 in. = 20.5 cm	60 in. = 152 cm

If you like these projects, you'll love these other fun craft booklets.

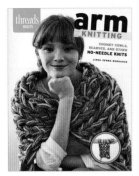

Arm Knitting
Linda Zemba Burhance
EAN: 9781627108867,
8½ × 10⅞, 32 pages,
Product #078045, $9.95 U.S.

Super Simple Stick Weaving
Ashley Little,
EAN: 9781631861598,
8½ × 10⅞, 32 pages,
Product # 078058, $9.95 U.S.

Bungee Band Bracelets & More
Vera Vandenbosch,
EAN: 9781627108898,
8½ × 10⅞, 32 pages,
Product # 078048, $9.95 U.S.

Mini Macrame
Vera Vandenbosch,
EAN: 9781627109574,
8½ × 10⅞, 32 pages,
Product # 078049, $9.95 U.S.

DecoDen Bling
Alice Fisher,
EAN: 9781627108874,
8½ × 10⅞, 32 pages,
Product # 078046, $9.95 U.S.

DecoDen Desserts,
Cathie Filian and Steve Piacenza,
EAN: 9781627109703,
8½ × 10⅞, 32 pages,
Product # 078053, $9.95 U.S.

Tie–Dye & Bleach Paint
Charlotte Styles,
EAN: 9781627109895,
8½ × 10⅞, 32 pages,
Product # 078055, $9.95 U.S.

Rubber Band Charm Jewelry
Maggie Marron,
EAN: 9781627108881,
8½ × 10⅞, 32 pages,
Product # 078047, $9.95 U.S.

Beautiful Burlap
Alice Fisher,
EAN: 9781627109888,
8½ × 10⅞, 32 pages,
Product # 078054, $9.95 U.S.

Shop for these and other great craft books and booklets online: www.tauntonstore.com

Simply search by product number or call 800-888-8286, use code MX800126
Call Monday-Friday 9AM – 9PM EST and Saturday 9AM – 5PM EST.
International customers, call 203-702-2204